BRITAIN IN OLD PHOTOGRAPHS

DARLINGTON
AT WORK & PLAY

CHARLIE EMETT

SUTTON PUBLISHING LIMITED

Sutton Publishing Limited
Phoenix Mill · Thrupp · Stroud
Gloucestershire · GL5 2BU

First published 1997

Title page photograph: J.W. Pease
(1828–1903), eldest son and second-born of
Joseph Pease and Emma Gurney's eight sons
and four daughters. Surrounding him are, left
to right, Sarah Charlotte Hodgkin, born 1858,
Maud Mary Pease, 1862, Mrs Helen Blanche
Pease, 1865, Lucy Ethel Foxton, 1867, and
Agnes Claudia Fox Wilson, 1870.

British Library Cataloguing in Publication Data
A catalogue record for this book is available from the
British Library.

ISBN 0-7509-1689-3

Typeset in 10/12 Perpetua.
Typesetting and origination by
Sutton Publishing Limited.
Printed in Great Britain by
Ebenezer Baylis, Worcester.

Housed in this magnificent building, which was officially opened in 1917, are the *Northern Echo*, the
Darlington and Stockton Times and the *Advertiser*, which reach hundreds of thousands of readers every week.
No other newspaper group in the north-east or North Yorkshire covers so much ground so
comprehensively.

CONTENTS

ACKNOWLEDGEMENTS

Very special thanks to Andrew Smith, editor of the *Northern Echo*, who allowed me to raid his picture library, to Jenny Needham, whose ability is only exceeded by her beauty, and to Jane Whitfield, guardian of the *Echo* archives, whose coffee tastes as good as she looks. Thanks, also, to Betty MacFall of Darlington Civic Theatre, for her enthusiasm and help, to Jane Dodsworth who somehow managed to transform my scrawl into something legible, to Rachel Paxton, who can recognise a good picture when she sees one, and to Anne Bennett, whose ability to charm birds out of trees turns working with Sutton Publishing into a pleasure. You are all beautiful people.

Hardinge Bridge was built by Cleveland Bridge and Engineering Co. Ltd, Darlington, in 1912. It is 5,894 feet long and crosses the Ganges in Bangladesh.

DELIVERY ADDRESS

Jane Elizabeth Porteus
DARLINGTON MANOR CARE
HOME
70 FALMER ROAD,
DARLINGTON

DL1 4AZ,
UNITED KINGDOM

Bookbarn International Ltd

Unit 1 Hallatrow Business Park, Wells
Road, Hallatrow,
Bristol
Somerset, BS39 6EX,
UNITED KINGDOM

Packing Slip / Invoice

Price: £6.97

Standard

Order Date:	18/01/2022
BBI Order Number:	1451900
Website Order ID:	202-1044846-3557151

Customer Contact: Jane Elizabeth Porteus

NOS1

NOS2

SKU InvID	Locators	Item Information
3634042 10894342	377-01-00 353948 Blue PAP ExLib - N U:G	**Darlington at Work and Play in Old Photographs (Britain in Old Photographs)** Emett, Charlie

If you wish to contact us regarding this order, please email us via Amazon quoting your order number.

amzuk

Thanks for shopping with us

www.bookbarninternational.com

1451900

 **bookbarn**
read | reuse | recycle

Greetings from Bookbarn!

Thank you so much for placing an order with us, in doing so you've helped us grow as an independent bookseller.

We hope you're happy with your purchase, however if you have any issues or queries please do not hesitate to contact us.
Log into the website you bought from, locate your order in your order or purchase history and **Contact Seller.**
Our small and committed team provides a fast response to ensure you are fully satisfied.

Kind regards & happy reading!

The Bookbarn Team

ブックバーンからのご挨拶！

ご注文ありがとうございます、
そうすることで、あなたは私たちが
独立した書店。

ご購入にご満足いただければ幸いです。
問題や質問がある場合はしないでください
お気軽にお問い合わせください。

購入したウェブサイトにログインし、
注文または購入履歴で注文を見つけます
と販売者に連絡してください。

私たちの小さくて献身的なチームは、
あなたを確実にするための速い応答
完全に満足しています。

よろしく＆幸せな読書！
ブックバーンチーム

Salutations de Bookbarn !

Merci beaucoup d'avoir passé une commande avec nous, ce faisant, vous nous avez aidés à grandir en tant que libraire indépendant.

Nous espérons que vous êtes satisfait de votre achat, cependant si vous avez des problèmes ou des questions s'il vous plaît ne pas N'hésitez pas à nous contacter.

Connectez-vous au site Web sur lequel vous avez acheté, localiser votre commande dans votre historique de commandes ou d'achats et contactez le vendeur.

Notre petite équipe dévouée offre un réponse rapide pour vous assurer sont pleinement satisfaits.

Bien cordialement et bonne lecture !
L'équipe de la librairie

¡Saludos desde Bookbarn!

Muchas gracias por realizar un pedido con nosotros. al hacerlo, nos has ayudado a crecer como líbrero independiente.

Esperamos que esté satisfecho con su compra, sin embargo, si tiene algún problema o consulta, por favor no dude en contactarnos.

Inicie sesión en el sitio web en el que compró, ubica tu pedido en tu pedido o historial de compras y póngase en contacto con el vendedor.

Nuestro pequeño y comprometido equipo proporciona una respuesta rápida para asegurarle están completamente satisfechos.

Saludos cordiales y feliz lectura!
El equipo de Bookbarn

Grüße aus Buchbarn!

Vielen Dank für Ihre Bestellung bei uns, damit hast du uns geholfen, als ein zu wachsen unabhängiger Buchhändler.

Wir hoffen, dass Sie mit Ihrem Kauf zufrieden sind, aber wenn Sie haben irgendwelche Probleme oder Fragen bitte nicht zögere uns zu kontaktieren.

Melden Sie sich bei der Website an, auf der Sie gekauft haben, Suchen Sie Ihre Bestellung in Ihrer Bestell- oder Kaufhistorie und Verkäufer kontaktieren.

Unser kleines und engagiertes Team sorgt für ein schnelle antwort, um sicherzustellen, dass Sie sind voll zufrieden.

Liebe Grüße und viel Spaß beim Lesen!
Das Bookbarn-Team

UK +44 (0)1761 451 333 | bookbarn@bookbarninternational.com

INTRODUCTION

Darlington, the tun or homestead of Dearnop's people, is centred around St Cuthbert's Church and the market place on the sloping west bank of the River Skerne, close to its confluence with the River Tees. Its origins are Saxon. Ethelred the Unready gave permission for Darlington and its surrounding villages to be given to the religious community at Durham, which looked after St Cuthbert's relics, in about 1010. This is the earliest surviving record of Darlington's existence.

The Boldon Book of 1183 and a further survey 200 years later together show what life was like in medieval Darlington. Freeholders had to make money payments to the Bishop, while bond tenants provided services or payments in kind.

With the establishment of the Commonwealth in 1649, the Bishopric was abolished and the manors and courts of Darlington were placed under the control of Parliamentary trustees, who appointed the Bailiff. In 1660, with the restoration of Charles II, the old order was re-established; but by the beginning of the eighteenth century it was falling apart, and the responsibility for running the town was in the hands of just thirteen men.

Darlington's Board of Health, initially established to comply with the Public Health Act of 1848 to provide the town with an effective water supply and drainage system, gradually acquired more powers. In 1854 it obtained the right to buy the Town Hall and adjacent shambles, control the market and make bye-laws. In 1861 it was authorised to buy the Bailiff's office from the Bishop of Durham and take over the Burial Board's powers. This led to the letting out of lucrative contracts and to the plural voting system to which many people objected. The Board's activities led to some resentment from certain of the town's inhabitants who, in 1856, founded Darlington Ratepayers' Association, whose members vehemently opposed the Board's chairman, Joseph Pease (1799–1872).

In 1865, a meeting convened to discuss the possibility of Darlington becoming a Corporate Borough with a Mayor and elected representatives ended without a clear majority in favour of the motion. This intransigence generated enough criticism to prompt Joseph Pease to resign, which he did in September 1866, having been chairman of the Board of Health for eight years.

The following March, following a Parliamentary Commission's enquiry, Darlington got its charter and the first elections were held that December. The chosen representatives, three from each of the six wards and six aldermen, included five Peases. One, Henry Fell Pease (1838–96), was Darlington's first Mayor, and several former Board of Health members were also Peases, so the *status quo* was maintained. When Darlington became a Corporate Borough, it also acquired the right to elect its own MP. In the 1868 General Election, Edmund Backhouse, a Quaker and member of the former Board of Health, was elected as Darlington's first MP. In 1915, Darlington acquired County Borough status and, ever growing, today has twelve electoral wards.

The right to hold a market in Darlington dates from the late twelfth century. The Bishop of Durham held the charter, which gave him a steady income. The tolls were collected by the Bailiff, the only people exempt being Darlington's freeholders. The Borough Court determined how the market was conducted and the quality of the goods sold. The trading area was clearly defined and dealing elsewhere was forbidden. The ringing of a market bell opened trading and anyone starting before it rang was fined.

By the sixteenth century, Darlington had a regular Monday market day and special fairs throughout the year. The cattle market was held in Bondgate until 1876 when a new one was opened near the top of Victoria Road.

The manufacture of woollen goods in Darlington lasted from 1183 until its decline almost 700 years later. During the mid-eighteenth century the town had a thriving leather industry, with tanneries lining the Skerne. The town was also renowned for the fine quality of the linen goods it produced. In 1790, an ironmonger's shop opened in Tubwell Row; it eventually became world renowned in the field of heavy engineering. Until recently this firm, Whessoe, was Darlington's largest employer. So Darlington had been an industrial town long before the Stockton & Darlington Railway was built in 1825.

The coming of the railways stimulated the town's economy. William Lister set up two iron foundries and William Kitching moved to larger premises and began making locomotives. In 1863, Shildon works, already providing and maintaining the S & D Railway's locomotives and rolling stock, opened engine building and repair shops in North Road: in 1868, Fry, I'anson and Co. opened rolling mills and in 1877 the Cleveland Bridge and Engineering Co. came into being.

People began to think of Darlington as a 'railway town', but it was also a 'newspaper town' because it was the only place in England to publish and distribute a daily paper with a circulation far in excess of the town's population. The *Northern Echo* was first published on Saturday 1 January 1870. Darlington was chosen as its headquarters thanks to its excellent railway communications, which allowed the newspaper to be sold simultaneously in London and Edinburgh. Its sales, on launch, were 10,000 copies a day, and from its inception the *Northern Echo* was a regional newspaper in the widest possible sense. In 1871, W.T. Stead, who went on to become the most famous journalist of his day, became its editor. Prime Minister W.E. Gladstone once told him: 'To read the *Echo* is to dispense with the necessity of reading other papers: it is admirably got up in every way.' Today's editorial team continues to ensure that Mr Gladstone's comment is still applicable; and if circulation figures are a criterion, Mr Stead will be smiling and nodding approval.

Darlington people work hard and play hard. Their football team, 'The Quakers', has a devoted supporters' club, as does the cricket team. Cricket has been played in Darlington since Victorian times by all classes of society. Bowls is also very popular. There is one cinema with three screens. Exciting happenings take place regularly at the Arts Centre, while the Dolphin Centre is second to none for excellence in sport. There are numerous pubs and clubs, catering for all tastes; but the jewel in Darlington's crown is its Civic Theatre, the most successful provincial theatre in the country. Moreover this modern, thriving town has easy access to some of England's most beautiful countryside. Much of the squalor of the Industrial Revolution depicted in this book has gone. Today's Darlingtonians lift their heads in pride, walk with a jaunty step, laugh a lot and smile at the world, perhaps a little smugly. For the town centre is ablaze with colourful flowers.

SECTION ONE

THE QUAKER TOWN

Founded by George Fox, a Leicestershire weaver, the Society of Friends, known as the Quakers because on a memorable occasion Fox, on trial, told the judge to 'tremble in the name of the Lord', has as its basis the guiding presence of the Holy Spirit in the heart of everyone. Before the Act of Tolerance of 1689, meetings were held at private houses. The first reported meeting of Darlington Quakers was in 1666 at the house of Dorothy Thompson. Before then, meetings were held in nearby villages such as Heighington. This is an early meeting house in Darlington.

In 1768, land was obtained by the Society of Friends to build a larger meeting house behind Skinnergate. This sketch of the proposed frontage is dated 1840.

The meeting house façade matches the sketch exactly. The Society of Friends, founded in 1648, had a profound effect on the prosperity of Darlington, which became known as the Quaker town. Many of the town's houses and public buildings that were built or remodelled during the eighteenth and nineteenth centuries were the outcome of Quaker involvement in commerce and banking, where they prospered.

The interior of Darlington's Friends' Meeting House. The Quaker religion is founded on silent prayer: there is no minister, no set service, no hymns. Anyone who feels prompted by the Holy Spirit may speak. Friends are pacifists because their aim is to bring light to evil minds, not to destroy them. Friends regard the Bible as of great importance for understanding the will of God, but not as the final authority.

There are no special sacraments such as baptism or the Lord's Supper. Church government is shared equally by all members of the meeting. Elders are appointed to arrange meetings and overseers to undertake pastoral work. In wartime they devote themselves without discrimination to bringing relief to the suffering.

The persecution of Nonconformist sects in England in the seventeenth century caused many Friends to emigrate to the colony of Pennsylvania, founded by the great Quaker William Penn, in 1862, and to other American colonies.

In 1947, the Nobel Peace Prize was awarded jointly to the American Friends' Service Committee and the British Friends' Service Council for their work towards international reconciliation. Philanthropy is considered a natural part of personal piety and has found expression through famous reformers and movements: the American, John Woolman (1720–72) and the struggle against slavery; Elizabeth Fry and prison reform; Joseph Rowntree (1801–59) and George Cadbury and social reform in industry. Membership of the Society of Friends is worldwode.

This austere scene, part of the Quaker cemetery, is seen from Powlett Street. All men are equal in God's eyes, so all the headstones are exactly the same size.

A conventicle originally meant a secret meeting among groups of monks. The word was later used as a term of reproach for meetings of Nonconformists in England and Wales in the seventeenth century. The Conventicle Act of 1664, repealed by the Toleration Act of 1689, made a gathering of more than five people for the purpose of worship other than according to the Book of Common Prayer a punishable offence.

Darlington's Friends suffered greatly, were heavily fined and had their goods confiscated. The vicar of St Cuthbert's Church, Revd George Bell, even allowed one Edward Boyes to sit in the church's organ loft to give him a better view of who was or was not attending the service. As a consequence of this, many Friends and other dissenters were subjected to brutal behaviour by drunks who, as the Darlington Quaker Book of Suffering records, terrorised even the infirm and the weak. Behind those headstones are some despicable stories of intolerance. Edward Pease, 'Father of Railways', who was born in 1767 and died on 31 July 1858, is buried in the Quaker cemetery.

THE URBAN ENVIRONMENT

The Pease family were leading Quaker members of nineteenth-century Darlington society. This sketch shows the unveiling of a statue of Joseph Pease, 1875. The man with his hand on the barrier is His Grace, the 4th Duke of Cleveland, who unveiled it.

The unveiling of Joseph Pease's statue at the northern end of High Row on 28 September 1875 was the highlight of the town's celebrations to commemorate the fiftieth anniversary of the opening of the Stockton & Darlington Railway. It was erected in recognition of his extraordinary ability and his tremendous efforts to boost the town's economy. He was the first Quaker to represent Darlington in Parliament; he was also one of the founders of the S & D Railway line, which marked the beginning of the expansion of trade and industry throughout the land.

A crowd throngs High Row to witness the unveiling of Joseph Pease's statue. Every vantage-point is occupied. The tall building on the left is today's Barclays Bank.

Joseph Pease, born on 22 June 1799, was the second son of Edward Pease, the 'Father of Railways'. He died on 8 February 1872, having distinguished himself as a successful industrialist and a Liberal MP, much involved with most aspects of Darlington life. He was married to Emma Gurney and they had eight sons and four daughters. His statue was designed by Joseph Lawson of London. It was originally graced with four stylish circular lamps on slim stands, one at each corner.

A few years later, the lamps had been removed, only the wider bases of the stands, now attached to low metal railings, remaining. Dresser, behind the statue, has burgeoned into one of the town's most impressive stores, now known as Dressers. Joseph Pease is depicted looking along the cobbles between High Row and Prebend Row, southwards. At that time, in 1875, cattle, sheep and horses were auctioned on those cobbles every Monday. In 1897 Darlington Council offered £20 for the best means of improving the area. A Mr Roberts won the prize but his idea was never used. Instead, the council adopted a scheme by the town surveyor which entailed removing the cobbles and consolidating the area by building it up behind steps. The work was completed in 1901.

An ornamental lamp, originally erected close to the Shambles to commemorate the coronation of King William IV, was moved from the Market Place in 1862 to make way for a new market hall. Its new home was in front of Prospect Place, the original site of Joseph Pease's monument, shown in this picture with four lamps.

When, on inviting the 4th Duke of Cleveland to unveil the Joseph Pease statue in the presence of the Lord Mayors of London and York, Alderman Luck, chairman of the committee which had commissioned the statue, assured everyone that the statue would be handed down to the Mayor and Corporation of Darlington 'with every confidence that it would be carefully protected and handed down to posterity'. It very nearly wasn't. In 1958 the statue was removed to ease the traffic flow. Three months later it was re-sited nearby, where it stands today; but only after some council chamber opposition.

The statue's plinth carries four scenes, each depicting a different aspect of life in 1875. This one shows a schoolteacher teaching a class of standing children the rudiments of English grammar.

This scene shows gratitude being expressed to one of William Wilberforce's slavery abolitionists. Guess who? Joseph Pease, a member of the anti-slavery movement.

Joseph Pease in the lobby of the House of Commons with Lord Palmerston, Lord John Russell and other prominent parliamentarians.

This set piece celebrates the coming of steam, and shows industries associated with the Pease family.

Joseph Pease bought this house in 1826. Called Southend, it was built by Edward Blackhouse. Pease extended the house and, following his death in 1872, his daughters continued to live there. When the last of them died in 1895, the house was taken over by the Catholic School of the Immaculate Conception. In 1975, it became the Grange Hotel.

Here the Peases could relax. The fountain and the private lake soothed generations of this extraordinary Quaker family.

Joseph Whitwell Pease was caricatured in *Vanity Fair*, 1887.

The eldest son of Joseph Pease, the first Quaker MP, he was born on 23 June 1828, at Southend, the family mansion in Darlington. On reaching seventeen he joined the family's enormous business empire and quickly became an important figure, developing mines all over the north-east and building railways to serve them. In 1865 he became MP for South Durham, the same constituency his father had retired from in 1841. When political boundaries were redrawn in 1885, he chose the Barnard Castle area of South Durham as his own and was always re-elected as a Liberal with good majorities. He was given a baronetcy in 1882; and twenty years later disaster struck. In 1902, the family bank of J.W. Pease crashed. It was an exclusive bank where account holders had to be members of the Pease family, although a few leading north-eastern companies were allowed to use the bank's services. So, when the bank crashed, much of the strength of the Pease empire went down too. The strain severely affected Sir Joseph's health. Six months later, in Falmouth, he died suddenly of heart failure. It was his seventy-fifth birthday. At the time of his death, he was Father of the House of Commons, having served the same constituency for the greatest number of years.

The centre of the town, so beloved of the Pease family, is seen silhouetted against the setting sun, December 1973.

The town clock was a gift from Joseph Pease. Built by Cooke of York, it cost £1,000, a lot of money in 1864 when it was fixed to the tower of the market hall. Because the original gilt hands were difficult to distinguish against the coloured dial, it was suggested to Joseph Pease that black hands against a white background would be more practical. He agreed, and the change was made.

Darlington's municipal regalia comprises the Mayor's chain of office (double strand), the Mayoress's chain of office (single strand) and the mace.

This rather splendid street lamp is always placed outside the home of the current mayor. It adds a touch of class, but does not always receive the respect it deserves.

When, because of failing health, Joseph Pease declined the honour of being Darlington's first mayor, it was transferred to Henry Fell Pease. Mr Hugh Dunn was the first town clerk. The Charter of 1867 enabled 'the people of the town to play a real part in its affairs'. One clause in it states: 'The inhabitants of the said town of Darlington and their successors shall be for ever hereafter one body politic and corporate in deed, fact and name, and the said body shall be called the Mayor, Aldermen and Burgesses of the Borough of Darlington.' Another decreed that the borough 'shall and may have Armorial Bearings and Devices which shall be duly entered and enrolled in the Heralds' College'. The first arms of the borough, however, were unofficial and unregistered. They remained so until 1960 when Darlington finally became heraldically respected.

This is the new medallion on the mayoress's chain of office, 1962.

The Quakers put great emphasis on education, seeing it as the solid foundation on which to build a rich and fulfilling life. G.G. Hoskins designed the Technical College, opened in 1897, in Northgate. The Bulmer Stone on the pavement was moved inside the railings in June 1923, having become a traffic hazard.

Darlington College of Further Education, designed by J.W. Pritchett, was opened in 1872. It sent out teachers to many parts of the world and welcomed students from overseas. In 1978, it closed as a college and has become the town's Art Centre.

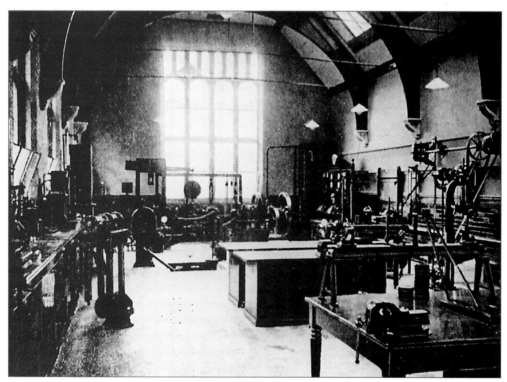

When Darlington College of Further Education was built, it was called a white elephant, but so many attended that between 1905 and 1910 extensions had to be built.

Maureen Hodge of Edinburgh College of Art assists Ruth Cordingley at Darlington College of Education, July 1975.

Darlington became a County Borough in 1915 and this caused serious difficulties in the field of education. At first Durham County Council's interference in Darlington's affairs was beneficial. The Technical Instruction Act of 1889 empowered it to spread the proceeds of a penny rate on technical education, and from it the County provided Darlington Grammar School with a science lab and a chemistry master. It was also authorised to award extra scholarships to the school, something the Borough could not do. By 1900 the school depended on the County for about a quarter of its income. There were mutual advantages and few difficulties.

The Education Act of 1902 changed all that. Local school boards were abolished and Darlington Council took control of elementary education, but secondary and technical schools passed into the hands of the County. This presented no serious problems for the Girls' High School, whose governing body remained unchanged. The transfer went smoothly. However, the County was no longer prepared to subsidise the Grammar School, as it had done, without having a larger share in its management. In 1906, an attempt was made to bring the Grammar School within the general scheme for secondary education for Durham whereby the County would assume complete control and fees would be reduced to £4 10s per annum. The governors struggled to remain independent, the County refused to budge and the school's financial position weakened. This impasse was finally broken when the County overspent on education, making the prospect of full control and the increased expenditure it entailed no longer an attractive proposition.

The rapid expansion of engineering in Darlington had stimulated a demand for suitable education facilities. So the Town Council, industrialists and other interested parties combined to establish a Technical College. It opened in 1897; but since the Education Act of 1902 decreed it, the venture was handed over to Durham, the governors becoming a subcommittee of the County Council. This led to a deterioration of relations between the subcommittee and the County Council. With time, administrative difficulties arose but the real problem was the principle at stake. Darlington was growing and needed the College, which was forging strong links with industry. The County, facing increasing education costs, wanted to limit expenditure. The Town Council requested a new, experimental steam boiler for the College. The County quibbled, so providing the Town Council with the determination to become independent.

In 1874, the Free Grammar School of Queen Elizabeth was opened, financed by many contributions, including £6,000 from the Pease family. It became the town's sixth-form college in 1970.

A study bedroom at Darlington Training College, 1936.

An aerial view of Duke Street, looking westwards. The tall building on the skyline is the Grammar School.

Darlington's expansion towards Cockerton on its western side really began in about 1901 with the building of much terraced housing on land that had originally belonged to the Pease family. The grounds of their mansion, Southend, became smothered beneath this large housing development. Not so Green Park and the land between Grange Road and Southend Avenue, today famed for its springtime display of crocuses, all of which were saved. In the late 1930s, when the Pierremont and the Brinkburn estates were broken up and sold, large-scale house building started in the area between the town and Cockerton. But the strip of land alongside Cocker Beck was preserved as a park.

The west end of Duke Street with the Grammar School in the background.

The horse shown in this sketch of the east end of Duke Street is walking along Skinnergate. The name Duke Street refers to the owner of the land on which it was built, as do nearby Vane Terrace and Stanhope Road. By 1870 a start had been made on the building of middle-class housing on land belonging to the Duke of Cleveland, west of Skinnergate.

Mid-nineteenth-century Darlington had a serious vagrancy problem; some 44,000 itinerants passed through the town annually. The more fortunate ones, those able to pay for a bed, stayed in one of Skinnergate's common lodging houses.

Horsemarket, late nineteenth century. Bailey's Printing Works later became W.H. Smiths and the Old English Tea Rooms.

Horsemarket, *c.* 1930. St Cuthbert's Church is at the far end and the Old Town Hall is on the left.

High Northgate, 1920. The lady cyclist doesn't fancy the man behind, who doesn't fancy her friend, who is trying hard not to lose him!

Turn-of-the-century Northgate with, on the left, the Theatre Royal where, on Monday 4 November 1901, Miss Maud Darling (see p. 35) thrilled her hometown audience as the 'Belle of New York'.

This view looks along High Northgate, away from the town centre, *c.* 1900. Snow has transformed the scene into an urbanised version of a Breughel painting.

Bulmer's Stone, deposited by a retreating glacier, remained on Northgate's pavement until June 1923, when it was moved behind the Technical College railings.

The Ivy Cottage, Northgate, was built by one of the I'anson family in about 1800. Mr N. Backhouse bought it between 1808 and 1815 and died there in 1844. Mr Beaumont Pease bought it in 1854, after which it was let to several tenants before becoming School Board offices, the Liberal Unionist Club and offices of Mr E.W. Lyall, Civil Engineer. In 1908, most of the ivy was cut down and the real long-term tenants, a colony of starlings, evicted.

EAST ELEVATION of EDWARD PEASE'S HOUSE.
NORTHGATE.

On 19 April 1821, the day the Stockton & Darlington Railway Bill received Royal Assent, Edward Pease, the 'Father of Railways', held a meeting at his Northgate home with George Stephenson and Nicholas Wood, at which Stephenson's application to be the engineer to build the line was discussed. Also, for the first time, the use of locomotives was mooted.

NORTHGATE — DARLINGTON

These houses were demolished in 1865 to make way for Pease's new house.

Northgate, *c.* 1870. Until 1786, when they purchased two houses in Bondgate for worship, Darlington's small Roman Catholic population celebrated mass in a large room in Northgate.

Northgate, looking towards High Row, 1908. The short stretch of double track is a passing point for trams.

Northgate, 1920. The tall building on the left, faintly seen, is the Technical College, built in 1897 and called at the time 'Darlington's latest white elephant'. It was designed by George Gordon Hoskins, who also designed the Edward Pease Public Library, the New Hippodrome and Palace of Varieties Theatre, now the Civic Theatre, and other buildings in Darlington and Middlesbrough. The College's original intake of pupils was 564, but demand for places quickly overtook supply and extensions had to be built in 1905 and 1910 to cope with it.

Darlington post office, Northgate, 1868.

Prebend Row or Low Flags lies at the centre of Darlington. Once it was a sunny bank where blackberries grew in profusion.

William 'Saddler' Watson, whose corner shop is in the centre, had a daughter, Maud (1881–1927) who changed her name to Darling, after the town, and became the internationally renowned actress Maud Darling.

In the 1890s, Darlington was a bustling market town, as this picture shows. The street on the left in the foreground is Priestgate.

Trolley-buses have replaced Darlington's trams. This picture dates from the 1930s.

Priestgate in afternoon sunshine, 1900. Ladies in ankle-length dresses, the horses and the chimney skyline combine to bring life and excitement to this bustling scene.

Darlington Union Workhouse, edging Yarm Road, has now been demolished and the stigma attached to it and all workhouses is no more. In its day, it served Darlington well. Now its responsibilities have been adopted by the welfare state.

Today Yarm Road is one of the town's main arteries. Once it was a rustic lane of great charm.

The Stone Bridge is seen here, three-arched and rather beautiful, 1767. St Cuthbert's Church is little changed but the River Skerne is now contained within man-made barriers.

Stone Bridge now has buildings adjacent to it, 1891. Darlington is growing.

Blackwell Bridge crosses the River Tees on the western edge of town.

Bonomi's Bridge, which carried the first railway coaches on the S & D line, has taken a battering from the Industrial Revolution.

Station Bridge, seen here in about 1930, before it was widened. Yarm Road goes under the bridge and immediately bifurcates, Yarm Road keeping straight ahead eastwards, Neasham Road forking right. St John's Church stands in the 'V' of the fork. Built to accommodate the spiritual needs of the area surrounding Bank Top station, which was developing fast, it was financed, for the most part, by the subscriptions of the railway shareholders. It opened for worship in 1850. That is the reason usually given; but, in fact, it was built because a Carpenter was looking for joiners.

THE RAILWAY TOWN

Dobbin's watercolour of the formal opening of the Stockton & Darlington Railway. The train is crossing the River Skerne on Bonomi's Bridge.

A train lets off steam at Bank Top Station, February 1931. Like our earliest castles, the original station at Bank Top was made of wood. In fact, it was just an untidy wooden shed. Queen Victoria was not amused by its shabby appearance when she visited Darlington on 28 May 1849. She pointed out that for the main line station of the very place in which the railways had been born to look so down at heel was not good enough. Someone should see to it that something was done about it. The Great North of England Railway, whose station it was, made some improvements. But thirty-eight years were to pass before, in 1887, Bank Top station was built at a cost of £110,000. When, during the Second World War, weak tea, rock hard rock buns and sandwiches with curled edges were sold at the station buffet, battle-hardened members of His Majesty's Forces followed the now late queen's example and complained vociferously.

The south end of Darlington Bank Top shows the locomotive depot in 1938 at the time of its reconstruction.

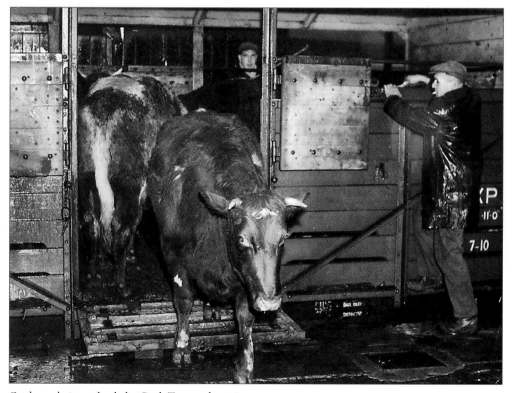

Cattle are being unloaded at Bank Top goods station.

This composite photograph shows Locomotion No. 1 on platform one, at Bank Top station. On 10 September 1825, Locomotion No. 1 was drawn by horses from Newcastle to Aycliffe Lane, Heighington, where it was placed on the railway line to complete its first journey to Darlington under its own steam. It had been built that same year by Robert Stephenson and Co., cost £500 and was the first locomotive owned by the Stockton & Darlington Railway Company. For twenty-five years it was used on the S & D Railway before being bought by Joseph Pease and Partners, who used it in their collieries until 1857 when it went into retirement, displayed on a plinth outside Darlington's North Road station. There it remained for a further thirty-five years. In 1892 it was moved to Bank Top station and placed on another plinth at the end of a bay at the south end of the station. It is now in the Railway Museum, Darlington.

THE NEWSPAPER TOWN

Proud leaders of a noble profession, these dedicated editors and those who followed them have established a provincial newspaper that, nationally, has gone on to produce Industrial Journalist of the Year, top awards for young journalists, photography and sports coverage and won nine of the sixteen awards in the North-East Press Awards in a single year, 1990. This healthy fashion continues and all the north-east and North Yorkshire benefit.

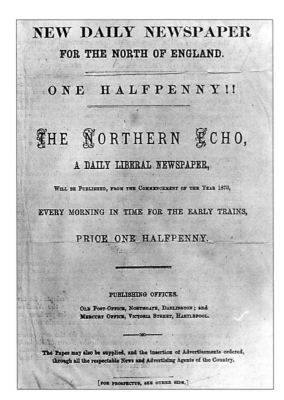

The birth of a newspaper giant is announced, 1870. W.T. Stead wrote:

'To give utterance to the inarticulate moan of the voiceless is to let light into a dark place; it is almost equivalent to the enfranchisement of a class. A newspaper in this sense is a daily apostle of fraternity, a messenger who bringeth glad tidings of joy, of a great light that has risen up on those who sit in darkness and the shadow of death.'

The first halfpenny morning paper in the world, Monday 12 January 1903.

The *Northern Echo* was founded in 1870 by J. Hyslop Bell, who insisted that the paper must sell for just a halfpenny so that it was available to everyone. Its first editor, W.T. Stead, was appointed in 1871. This outstanding newspaperman with printer's ink in his veins went on to become the most famous journalist of his day. Sadly, he went down with the *Titanic*. In 1895, E.D. Walker became sole proprietor of the *Northern Echo*. Production methods were modernised, new presses installed and the newspaper enlarged. In 1903, Walker sold the paper to the newly formed North of England Newspaper Co. Ltd, which was backed by the Joseph Rowntree Social Service Trust. The chairman was Arnold S. Rowntree and the manager was Charles W. Starmer. Under their control the *Northern Echo* became the foremost newspaper in the region.

This proud proclamation is made from the *Echo*'s original home.

The year the paper was first published, 1870, was also the year of Forster's Education Act, which was to bring into being a new generation of educated working-class people. A group of far-sighted northern businessmen decided to 'supply a want of the age and district, viz a well-conducted, high class Daily Newspaper advocating liberal opinions and published at a price which will bring it within reach of all classes of people.' Thus the *Northern Echo* was conceived.

Like the much-loved children's hymn, the *Northern Echo* is 'New every morning' from its first home, a modest terrace in Priestgate. From the outset it was a popular paper, and for almost a decade Stead's leader articles were read avidly by readers throughout the country. Liberal Prime Minister W.E. Gladstone once told him: 'To read the *Echo* is to dispense with the necessity of reading other papers; it is admirably got up in every way.'

Harry Burton of Fairville Road, Stockton, reading the 1914 *Northern Echo* that he found lining a drawer in his new home, 1987.

Huts were situated on the corner of Crown Street before 1915. This was to be the site of the *Echo*'s new home.

The scaffolding is up and the building is taking shape, January 1915. On the left is a soldier, probably on leave.

Most of the scaffolding has been removed, 1915. The one-horse-power rubble remover, centre, is backed up to the main entrance of the building!

Born as a 'Liberal, Nonconformist and Free Trade' newspaper, the *Northern Echo* is, today, strictly independent of all political parties. It champions the causes of its readers, particularly those ill-equipped to resist strong forces in society.

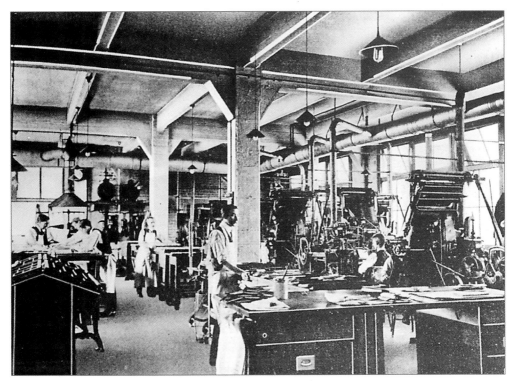

Linotype operators, 1917.

Sub-editors, 1917.

Early delivery vans, with the newspaper's name prominently displayed on two of them, *c.* 1917.

The editor's inner sanctum, *c.* 1917.

The compositing room, *c.* 1920. This is where the compositors set and corrected type. Until very recently newspapers were produced by the hot metal process, which involved fitting lines of metal type into a steel frame. This method had not changed for hundreds of years.

When the far-sighted Darlington businessman Edward Daniel Walker – nicknamed 'the W.H. Smith of the North' – became the sole proprietor of the *Northern Echo* in 1895, he made major technological changes. As well as installing additional printing presses, he made the *Echo* one of the first provincial newspapers to abandon the traditional process of typesetting by hand in favour of the much faster linotype keyboard method. In the same way, today's *Northern Echo*, *D & S Times* and *Advertiser* are in the forefront of the new technology which is revolutionising the newspaper industry. Nowadays most newspapers are photocomposed, which means that the hot metal type has been replaced with a photographic image. This is output via typesetting equipment on to photo-sensitive paper known as 'bromide'. This bromide process has now been abolished at Newsquest (North East) Ltd in favour of fully electronic page makeup on screen – the 'paperless' newspaper!

Northern Echo delivery vans, 1920. The front vehicle is advertising Nignogs, members of the *Northern Echo*'s children's circle, who perform charitable work for the children's hospital.

SWEET COMPANIONSHIP OF CHILDHOOD

Out of their compassion for the sick and suffering
and as a tribute to the noble work
of the Children's Hospital, the

———— NIGNOGS ————

Members of the Northern Echo Children's Circle
raised the funds to defray the cost of this

———— NIGNOG WARD ————

AND ENDOW THE COT

dedicating them in loving kindness to all little ones
afflicted by illness or accident

1932

Sweet companionship of childhood: the Nignogs, 1932.

Northern Despatch

DARLINGTON, THURSDAY, 10 DECEMBER, 1936. ONE PENNY

No. 6,756

LATE FINAL

ABDICATION OF KING EDWARD VIII

KING EDWARD THE VIII.

I HAVE DETERMINED TO RENOUNCE THE THRONE
— KING EDWARD'S MESSAGE

Task Grown Too Heavy For Him to Discharge with Efficiency

DUKE OF YORK BECOMES KING

Momentous Announcements Read by Speaker to Packed House

THE NEW KING

KING EDWARD THE VIII.

HISTORY OF THE CRISIS

How the Drama Unfolded from Day to Day

King Edward the VIII. has abdicated and the Duke of York succeeds to the Throne.

The Speaker made this momentous announcement in the House of Commons at 3.45 this afternoon. There was a packed assembly, which included Ambassadors and diplomats representing nearly every country in the world.

The message from King Edward was in the following terms:—

"After long and anxious consideration I have determined to renounce the Throne to which I succeeded on the death of my father, and I am now communicating this, my final, and irrevocable decision.

"Realising as I do the gravity of this step I can only hope that I shall have the understanding of my peoples in the decision I have taken, and the reasons which have led me to take it.

"I will not enter into my private feelings, but I would beg that it should be remembered that the burden which constantly rests upon the shoulders of a Sovereign is so heavy that it can only be borne in circumstances different from those in which I now find myself.

"I conceive that I am not overlooking the duty that rests on me to place in the forefront the public interest when I declare that I am conscious that I can no longer discharge this heavy task with efficiency or with satisfaction to myself.

"I have accordingly this morning executed an instrument of a decree of abdication in the terms following:—

"I, Edward the VIII. of Great Britain, Ireland, and the British Dominions beyond the Seas, King, Emperor of India, do hereby declare my irrevocable determination to renounce the Throne for myself and for my descendants, and most desire that effect should be given to this instrument of abdication immediately.

"In token whereof I have hereunto set my hand this tenth day of December, Nineteen hundred and thirty-six, in the presence of the witnesses whose signatures are subscribed." EDWARD, R.I.

"My execution of this instrument has been witnessed by my three brothers, their Royal Highnesses the Duke of York, the Duke of Gloucester, and the Duke of Kent.

"I deeply appreciate the spirit which has actuated the appeals which have been made to me to take a different decision, and I have reached my final determination most fully pondered over them.

"But my mind is made up. Moreover, further delay cannot but be most injurious to the peoples whom I have tried to serve as Prince of Wales and as King, and whose future happiness and prosperity are the constant wish of my heart.
Continued in Page 10.

TENSION IN THE HOUSE

DIPLOMATS PRESENT

The King's Abdication

HOW THE NEWS WAS RECEIVED
See Tomorrow's
Northern Echo

On The Horizon

The NEW Binns

Binns Limited
DARLINGTON

National news and local advertising share the front page of the *Northern Despatch*, a sister paper to the *Northern Echo*, 10 December 1936.

The delivery fleet: *Northern Despatch* on the left, *Echo* on the right, 1950.

Celebrating a century of service to the community, an event marked by a visit to the *Northern Echo* offices by Princess Anne.

AT WORK

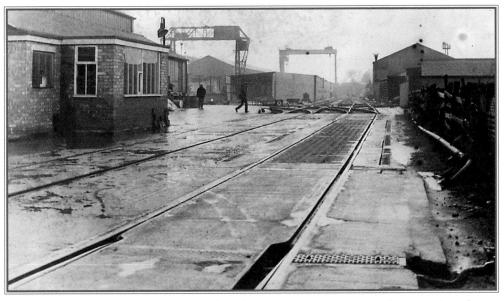

Until Cleveland Bridge and Engineering Co. Ltd moved to its current premises, this was the hub of its worldwide operations, off Neasham Road.

Cleveland Bridge's first overseas bridge in New South Wales, Australia, seen during construction, 1893.

Work in progress over the River Humber as a road section of the world's longest single-span suspension bridge is moved into position. With a main span of 4,625 feet, the Humber Bridge is 366 feet longer than the Verrazano Narrows Bridge in New York and 425 feet longer than the Golden Gate Bridge in San Francisco. It links Hessle on the north bank with Barton-upon-Humber.

An artist's impression of the Thames Barrier. The steel gates and operating mechanisms were made by a consortium of Cleveland Bridge and Davy-Loewy. Cleveland also installed the gates.

Contractor, the first locomotive from North Road Shops, Darlington, 1864.

North Road Shops workmen are assembled just before the outbreak of the First World War.

This is the last steam locomotive to be built at North Road Shops, 1957.

A steam engine is being demolished in North Road Shops' scrapyard, June 1960.

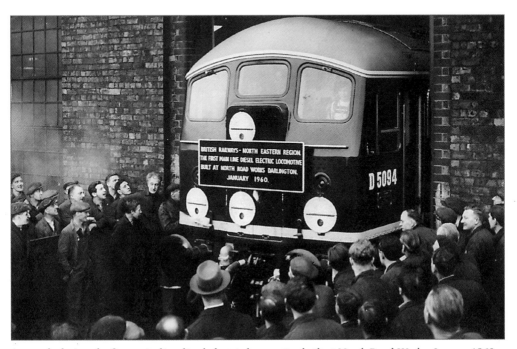

A crowd admires the first main-line diesel electric locomotive built at North Road Works, January 1960.

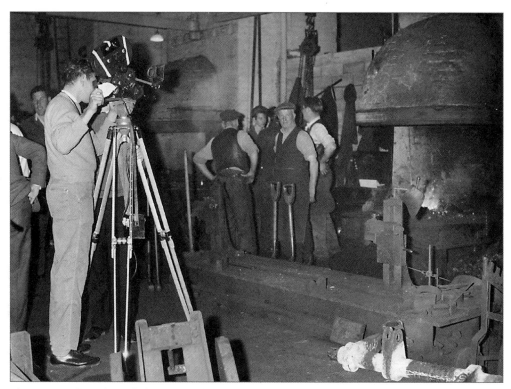

The interior of North Road Shops is seen being televised for the TV programme *Tonight*, 1962.

A mass demonstration against unemployment took place at North Road Shops, 27 March 1963.

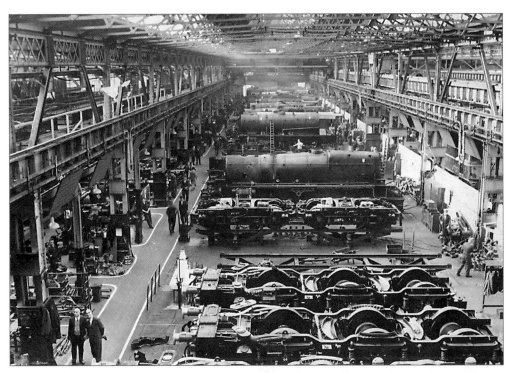

The interior of North Road Railway Workshops, Darlington, 1964. Engines are at various stages of production.

North Road Shops were first axed by Beeching in 1962 but won a stay of execution. Then, in 1965, the workforce learned that their deadline was 2 April the following year. Tom Hodgson, a semi-skilled machinist grade one, then aged fifty-seven and married with two girls and a boy still at school, commented: 'I've worked here 30 years and I'm wondering who will take me now. I'm looking round for a job already. The younger men lack the experience we have and industry needs a balance of young and old.' This was the man of whom a management representative said: 'In all the times I have been in this shop, I have never seen him away from his machine.'

A serious fire occurred at North Road Shops in 1973.

Founded in 1790, in its heyday Whessoe was Darlington's largest employer. This aerial view of the now demolished workshops and vacated offices shows the full extent of the firm's headquarters.

The first storage tank built by Whessoe for the Anglo-American Oil Company Ltd (later Esso), 1894. The tank had a capacity of 1,000,000 gallons.

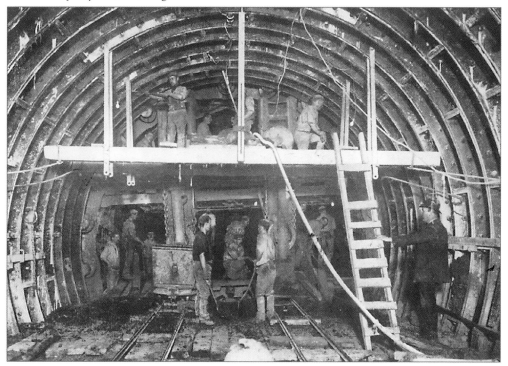

Work in progress, 1963. Whessoe supplied all the cast and wrought ironwork, amounting to about 50,000 tons, for the underground extension from Edgware Road to Baker Street and Waterloo stations.

This remarkable structure is thought to be the largest liquid ethylene storage sphere ever built. This double shell sphere was designed and built by Whessoe Ltd, at Esso's Fawley Refinery, 1964.

A huge pressure vessel leaves Whessoe's Darlington works bound for Saudi Arabia, 1964.

Darlington Cattle Market was opened near the top of Victoria Road in 1878. It marked the decline of selling livestock in the town centre. Beasts are shown in this picture, which means that on the following Monday it will be sheep.

Darlington Cattle Mart, *c.* 1930. Market day is still every Monday, with fair days for the sale of horned cattle and sheep being held on alternate Mondays from Whit Monday until Christmas.

A fine-looking beast is being paraded in the ring, 25 May 1964.

W. Carter's butcher's shop on Yarm Road remains a thriving business today. It has moved with the times, diversified somewhat, and the window displays are neater and more appealing.

Darlington's very own umbrella man had his business in Skinnergate in 1896. Such specialist shops are now almost as rare as hens' teeth.

James Rickaby stands outside his shop with his staff. He ran Rickaby's in Skinnergate from 1880 until 1910.

Walton's chemist's on the corner of Neasham Road and Albert Street is no more; the footbridge over the main east coast railway line remains, as does Bank Top station (on the left).

Fishmonger, poulterer and fruiterer Mr Barber has a nice business, established in Horsemarket, near the town centre, 1879. Next door is Adamson's Commercial Hotel & Dining Rooms.

It is 1896, and Mr Barber is no longer trading in Horsemarket. The shop next door has gained a bay window and become Calvert's Dining Rooms.

Darlington's covered market stalls are seen before the Second World War. Barber's is now long established, having had a shop in Horsegate in 1879.

It is 1920, the beginning of the Roaring Twenties, and S.M.Co. has the gear!

More than 300 years ago, an old house stood on the site occupied by J. Lear & Sons. It was the home of the Lambtons, then the Bowes family. Later Mr Samuel Booth, Mr Byers and Mr Thomas Furby lived there at various times, before Mr Lear occupied the site, establishing a brushmaking and hardware business there in 1706.

Gamble's cake shop, Duke Street, 1920. Guess whose chocolates *it* sells!

This shop is rather special; it is Darlington's first cop shop.

Dressers, 1985. In the 1890s the King's Head and Foxe's Oriental Café, Northgate, owners of private generators, were the first Darlington shops to have electric light. In December 1909 the Corporation's Haughton Road Works were generating electricity, an added attraction for Christmas shoppers in the town centre. In 1935 Darlington's electricity came from the national grid, from where Dressers gets its Christmas lights.

AT PLAY

Baydale Beck Inn, 1910. It is sited close to a probable chantry on the western edge of Darlington. The robber Sir William Brown used it as his headquarters — he was brought to trial and executed at Newcastle in 1743. Earlier, in 1624, one Christopher Simpson was murdered there and his ghost is reputed to haunt the old building. Dick Turpin is supposed to have used the inn, staying in a room with five doors for easy escape.

The Anchor Inn, run by Jimmy Coffey, was the quietest pub in town. Regulars had their accustomed seats and long pipes and it was considered reprehensible to use either a seat or pipe which another generally claimed.

The Black Lion is typical of the corner public house to be found in 1898 Darlington.

Thomas Bowser, a butcher, who died in 1842 aged seventy-one, was a former host of the Boot & Shoe, often called the Boot & Slipper, a pub frequented by leather workers, next door to the Hat & Feather. On 16 August 1809, he roasted an ox in the market place to commemorate the coming of age of the Earl of Darlington's heir.

James Philip was landlord of the Freemason's Arms from 1829 until 1834, when Dick Hedley, who had a blacksmith's shop in Priestgate, took over. In the construction of the older part of the building rushes were used instead of laths for the ceiling.

The Green Tree Inn, at the south end of Skinnergate, takes its name from a tree which stood outside. In 1924, the tree was felled, and in 1925 the inn closed. The Green Tree café is there now.

The Old Angel was adjacent to Blackwell School on the outskirts of town. The year is 1909, and the Law is on hand to take possession at the appointed hour.

The Leeds Arms Hotel, formerly the Rifle or Rifle Volunteer. A figure of a volunteer alongside a cannon was mounted on a small battery above the passage (left), level with the spouting. The hotel was closed in December 1909, and demolished the following year.

The Bay Horse Hotel stands at the corner of Albion Street. On one side of it Mr Barker had his draper's shop with, above it, the Liberal Association Clubrooms. On the other, Mr Warrener had his grocer's shop. The enlarged Bay Horse now covers both sites.

The Britannia Inn, 1960. This building has changed little outwardly since J.M. Dent, the eminent publisher, was born there.

The Fleece Hotel, 1960s. Built as the private residence of the Prescotts in the eighteenth century, it had 'a very ancient door studded and adorned with a cruciform knocker plate and fleur de lys' guarding its yard entrance. The building passed, by marriage, to the Pepper Arden family, and was sold to the Hird family in 1830. After three generations John Britton became landlord. In 1844, Joseph Forster bought it and installed its first tenant, John Lowson, who died, aged twenty-nine, in 1845. The hotel was demolished in 1968.

The Glittering Star's men's club outing to Scarborough, 1937. The lady at the front in the black dress is the landlady.

Feethams Field, 1905. This was once known as the prettiest part of town, but is now the site of Darlington FC. To the right lies the Skerne, with the Bishop's Mill (demolished in 1966) visible through the trees.

This medal was presented to Darlington players in recognition of cup progress, 1910–11.

Darlington Football Club, 1910–11 season.

Darlington FC, 1924–5. Players in the back row, left to right: Tom Greaves, Jimmy Crumley, Martin Joyce; middle row: Hughie Dickson, Ginger Robinson, George Malcolm; front row: Mark Hooper, William Hooper, Davy Brown, George Stevens, Tommy Winship. Trainer Shy Birch is on the extreme left with manager Jack English beside him. Chairman Robert Blaycock is seated on the right.

Beatrice Clacher of Middleton-St-George, 1982. Mrs Clacher holds a photograph of the team for the 1937–8 season in which her husband played.

The floodlighting creates a new landmark at Feethams, 19 September 1960. It is evincing interest from those present.

Darlington's first floodlit match, 19 September 1960.

The west stand ablaze, 20 September 1960.

Promotion smiles in the boardroom after Darlington's drawn game against Torquay, 23 May 1966. Left to right: Ald. J.A. Bird, Mr Lol Morgan (manager), Mr Harry Robinson (chairman), Mr Robin Holmes, Mr E. Blakeborough, Councillor H. Hannah (Mayor of Darlington) and Mr F.T. Walker. The cake, made in the shape of a football, was sent to St John of God Hospital at Scorton.

Darlington's first round FA cup tie
with Grimsby at Feethams,
18 November 1968. Lance Robson
finds himself sandwiched between
Lawton and Grimsby centre-half
Rathbone, but Macey (Grimsby
goalkeeper) manages to whip the ball
off Lawton's head.

Approaching Feethams with high pre-match expectations, April 1972. The cricket field is to the fore, left.
Trees line the Skerne.

Post-match reality.

Mr Leslie Moor, Chairman of Darlington Football Club, watches the first disabled Quaker fan go into the newly built enclosure, 1976. Standing by are members of the town's Rotaract Club.

A drawn game: Darlington 1, Halifax 1, 19 August 1976. So near and yet so far! Derek Craig (right) heads the ball inches over the bar while Eddie Rowles and Ron Ferguson look on in anguish.

Fans, 1977.   'How do you spell it?' *D-A-R-L-I-N-G-T-O-N*
                   'Who are the greatest?' *D-A-R-L-I-N-G-T-O-N*
                   'Who's going to Wembley?' *D-A-R-L-I-N-G-T-O-N*
But not this year: maybe next!

Gary Barden, seven, was knocked out by the ball when Darlington played Tranmere at home, 1980. He was made club mascot.

Quakers' Secretary, David Thorns, polishes up the Old Railway Relic above the tunnel at Feethams, 1981.

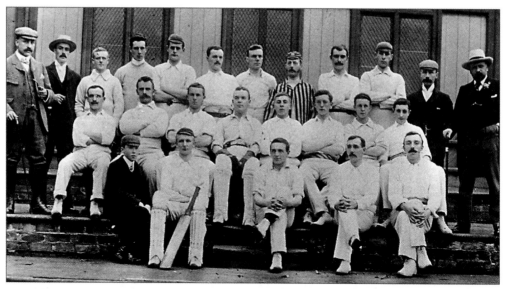

Darlington Cricket Club, 1902. That year A.P. Whitwell, fourth son of Quaker industrialist and Thornaby iron founder, William Whitwell, was captain of the first XI. He played for Yorkshire and Darlington in 1890, and was one of the very few Yorkshire cricketers born outside the county.

Darlington Seconds, who play in Division 3 of the North Yorkshire and South Durham Cricket League, 1976. Back row, left to right: J. Vart, R. Jackson, C. Bowes, A. Thompson, A. Johnson, J.E. Edwardson; front row: J. MacMillan, T. Dobson, C. Camburn, C. Harrison, J. Reynolds.

Net practice on Feethams cricket ground, 1971. Strictly, the batsman on the right cannot be bowled out: there are no bails on the stumps.

The Mayor of Darlington, Councillor Cliff Hutchinson, presents the Haith Trophy to Darlington Cricket Club Second XI captain, Mr G.B. Johnson, at the club dinner in the North Eastern Hotel, 1975. Club president, Mr R.A. Morton, looks on.

The Darlington Railway Athletic Team, which won the Kerridge Cup at Feethams, July 1973. Back row, left to right: John Drury, Richard Gent, Ken Wilkinson, John Rogers, John Buckman, Robert Davidson; front row: Peter Eckles, Walter Metcalfe, Tony Eckles (captain), David Whincup, Dudley Hughes.

The cricket section of the Darlington Railway Athletic Club in Brinkburn Road, Darlington, 1969.

North Lodge Park golfers proudly display their cup before heading for the 19th hole, *c.* 1930.

Darlington market place, on a pre-1900 Whit Monday Bank Holiday, complete with swing-boats and, to the left of them, a showman's skylight wagon.

A prehistoric monster, the Hospitaleffortamus, which gobbles money. This was an attraction at a pre-Second World War North Road Shops Carnival.

'Zulu' dancers, another popular attraction at the North Road Shops Carnival.

It's a hap-hap-happy day and carnival time, 1985. The annual Carnival Parade moves down Bondgate to the foot-tapping rhythms of the band.

The Beverley Sisters with beauty queen 'Miss Darlington 1967'. The sophisticated melody-makers smile their approval.

Terry Sutton, the Beer Festival Officer, tries a pint in the Arts Centre at the tenth Darlington Beer and Music Festival, 27 September 1989.

In 1882 a temporary bandstand was erected in South Park, near the lake. The girls are arriving for a pop concert 100 years too early!

Darlington clock tower in South Park, 1911. This was a more elegant age, when life moved at a gentler pace.

South Park lake, 1929. 'Come in No. 9. Oh, sorry! No. 6 has capsized!' Boating was a very popular activity at this time.

A floral design in South Park acknowledges the work of the WVS, June 1959.

The lake, South Park, February 1986. Canada Geese and other waterfowl prove they cannot read.

Nor can some humans, seen crossing the lake with a baby in a pram, January 1962. Perhaps they are just bird-brained?

The River Skerne in flood, March 1963.

Skating on South Park lake, 9 January 1969.

This South Park display recognises the great service the *Northern Echo* has contributed, not only to Darlington, but to the whole of the north-east.

The River Skerne in benign mood, flowing through South Park en route to its destiny with the River Tees, May 1979.

Darlington's North Road Museum, when the building was North Road station, and all the taxis were one horse-power!

Visitors to North Road Museum, complete with Victorian dress, board railway carriages dating back to the nineteenth century for a taste of bygone days, 1979.

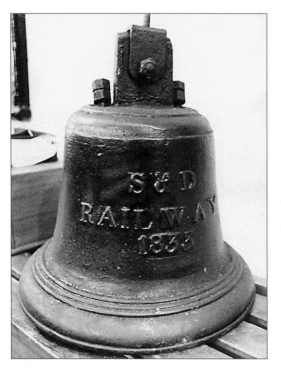

A bell inscribed S & D RAILWAY 1833, which was once rung to mark the beginning and the end of shifts.

A nineteenth-century Puffing Billy, one of the twenty similar models built at Darlington and Gateshead in 1885, now the first exhibit of North Road Museum.

A fireless locomotive from Patons (formerly Paton & Baldwins), the textile firm which used to run alongside the Stockton & Darlington Railway route. These locomotives were used in oil refineries and elsewhere where there was inflammable material. They were filled up with enough steam to keep them running for hours.

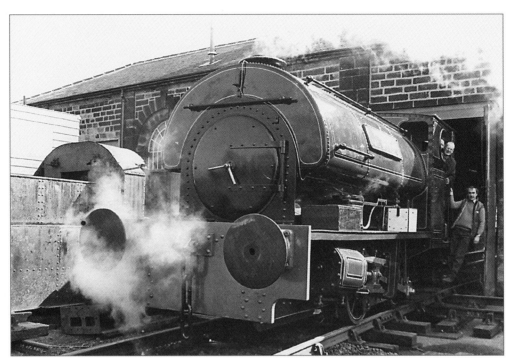

This Peckett engine, built in 1953, once served at Darlington gas works, and is now at North Road Museum.

A hat made for the Chief of Police, NE Area, and worn at the 1925 Centenary Celebrations. On the right is the container it was kept in.

The Alhambra, Northgate, boasted a complete orchestra for silent movies. Later the Alhambra became the Gaumont.

The Arcade Cinema, Skinnergate, which opened in 1912, was so successful that the following year a gallery was added.

The Astoria cinema, in High Northgate, near Station Road, later presented variety shows, attracting artists like Jack 'Mind my Bike' Warner before he became Dixon of Dock Green. The Denville Players Repertory Company, with Molly Sugden and Charles Simon among the cast, was based there. Then it became a bingo hall, then it went dark.

Despite its unprepossessing frontage, the Court Kinema was one of Darlington's most luxurious cinemas.

THE NORTHERN ECHO, WEDNESDAY, 12 FEBRUARY, 1913.

The Court Kinema, Darlington.

The Last Word in Kinema Perfection.

The interior of the Court Kinema, which really was the last word in 'Kinema Perfection' in 1913.

When the Rank Organisation purchased the Alhambra, it was renamed the Gaumont. Two chains of cinemas – Gaumont and Odeon-Rank – were controlled nationwide by Rank.

Darlington's first purpose-built cinema, the New Electric Picture Palace, 'the hall of 1,000 lights', opened in June 1911.

When the Majestic opened in December 1932, its seating capacity was 1,600 and it had an organ. This photograph shows it in the late 1940s.

When the Rank Organisation bought the Majestic, it was renamed the Odeon, a name kept until 1981 when it closed as a cinema. It is now a snooker hall. The queue here is for free tickets for senior citizens for the Christmas show, 10 December 1980.

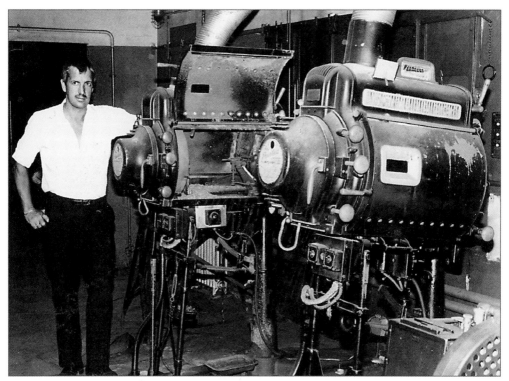

The projection room of the Regent cinema, Cobden Street, which was opened in June 1939. Later it was equipped with stereophonic sound, a dramatic innovation. Duncan Bannatyne stands by the projectors, 1987.

The Ritz, had it been built in 1936 as intended, would have brought Darlington's total of cinemas to ten. As it was, with nine working simultaneously, Darlington had more cinemas per head of population than any other town in the United Kingdom.

With the advent of television, cinema attendances fell dramatically. Many closed while others depended on ice cream sales to keep open. TV has developed into a mixed blessing with a tendency to make people anti-social. Not so radio, a much more amenable branch of the media. On 30 November 1995, Darlington got its own radio station, A1FM. Now called Alpha Radio, it broadcasts on a frequency of 103.2, has a range of about 12 miles and is a credit to the community it serves so well.

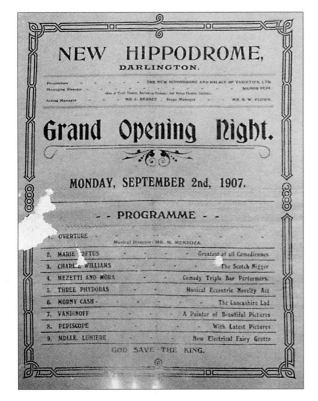

Programme for the Grand Opening Night of the New Hippodrome, 1907.

The New Hippodrome programme cover shows (inset) Signor Rino Pepi, the outstanding north-east entertainment personality, who guided the theatre's fortunes for many years.

On Monday 2 September 1907 the New Hippodrome and Palace of Varieties was formally opened in the presence of the Mayor and members of Darlington Corporation. It was a bold venture preceded by much debate because although Darlington's population was around 50,000 and local industry was growing, the town already had a theatre seating 1,000.

In April 1904, it was announced in the *D & S Times* that the Darlington Hippodrome Company Ltd had purchased from the Darlington Corporation a corner site in Parkgate adjacent to Borough Road. Capital of £30,000 was subscribed and the New Hippodrome was built within seven months by local contractor Mackenzie Bros. Mr George Gordon Hoskins designed the building and Mr G.F. Ward of Owen and Ward, who had built some twenty-five theatres and music halls in the north, supervised the construction work.

In 1861 Rino Pepi was born near Florence in Italy. He became a quick-change artist, was extremely popular on the continent and once appeared before Queen Victoria. He gave up performing at the height of his career, aged 41, and adopted a new career in theatre management. In 1902 he settled in the north-west where, at the Tivoli, Barrow-in-Furness, he pioneered the 'twice nightly' performance system. In 1907 he moved to Darlington where his company took the lease from the Darlington Opera House and Empire Ltd, which owned the Hippodrome's new and still incomplete development.

Signor Pepi quickly became an outstanding entertainment personality in the north-east and for many years guided the fortunes of the Darlington Hippodrome. He was a very popular, much-respected man of considerable charm and culture, noted for his generosity. Although at various times he held leases or financial interests in many music halls and theatres throughout the north, he only retained control of Darlington's Hippodrome when he died in 1927.

The New Hippodrome opened with a Grand Opening Night variety show starring Marie Loftus, 'greatest of comediennes', supported by a highly diverting cast. They played to a capacity audience of 1,210, seated on three levels; and the circle and gallery, being cantilevered, allowed all patrons an uninterrupted view of the stage, a large one, with a proscenium opening of 28½ feet and a depth of 32 feet. From it, the artistes looked on to a luxuriance of cream and gold, relieved with pale rose and turquoise blue ornamental plasterwork and drapes of crimson plush silk with gold appliqué trimmings. This was Edwardian splendour at its most opulent. Ninety years later and now called Darlington Civic Theatre, it has become the most successful provincial theatre in the country.

The great La Milo was appearing at the Hippodrome, 21 March 1910. The theatre is bedecked with bunting for the occasion.

A 1958 *Northern Despatch* cartoon comments on the birth of the Hippodrome as the Darlington Civic Theatre.

The Hippodrome theatre fills up for the visit of the Hallé Orchestra, 12 August 1960.

Champagne toasts the end of a wonderful evening, 30 January 1976. Theatre director, Peter Tod, second left, introduces Dame Margot Fonteyn to Mr R.A. Daniels, the managing director of the William Press Group of Companies, which co-sponsored the gala.

Lady Starmer, left, then president of Darlington Operatic Society, together with Eunice Cockburn and Peter Tod, the theatre director, on the occasion of the opening of the new boardroom, October 1977.

The theatre's original seating plan had a central aisle leading to the bar at the rear. This is how it looked from the stage in November 1982, before its major refurbishment.

During the alterations, all the stalls seats were removed. Even without seating, this proud, Edwardian theatre retains its touch of class.

The Civic's new seating arrangement. Removal of the centre aisle meant 'more bums on seats'. The curtain was purchased by the Friends of the Civic, who raised the necessary finance through prolonged, hard funding.

Having remained 'dark' for many years, the Hippodrome reopened as the Civic Theatre and a new canopy replaced the old one. This has since been replaced with an exact replica of the original one, and the theatre is the better for it.

The Civic Theatre, 1964. The façade is now as it was when built, except that the word 'Palace' has been removed from the rectangle on the right. A similar rectangle on the theatre's Borough Road wall had the word 'theatre' removed.

Entertaining Mr Sloane, one of the plays presented in the Civic's spring 1985 programme. Back: Peter Adamson and Frank Gatliff; front: Christopher Fulford and Pamela Sholto.

Once a Catholic brings laughter to the Civic Theatre.

Good Morning, Bill, by P.G. Wodehouse, with Richard Heffer as Bill and Mary Tamm as Sally, delighted Darlington audiences at the Civic.

The Northern Sinfonia in rehearsal for its concert at Darlington Civic Theatre. It presented all the Bach Brandenburg Concertos with which it made its Albert Hall Promenade concert debut.

Syd Lawrence and his Orchestra on stage at the Civic Theatre.

A scene from one of the ballets regularly presented at the Civic Theatre. Evenings of sheer enchantment!

The seventy-fifth birthday of the Civic Theatre was celebrated with a gala performance by Ken Dodd in the presence of the Mayor and Mayoress of Darlington, Councillor and Mrs William Newton, 2 September 1982. William MacDonald, director of the Civic Theatre, raises his glass while Ken Dodd attacks the cake.

Comedy actress Molly Sugden, holding a 'House Full' sign, always the aim of the Darlington Civic Theatre.

AT PRAYER

St Cuthbert's, 1760. The church is backed by the bottom of Tubwell Row, then dwellings set among trees. A nine-arched bridge spans the River Skerne and, beyond it, to the right, there is a mill.

The medieval parish church of St Cuthbert, 1843. Its churchyard was Darlington's only burial ground until the 1670s when the Quaker burial ground was opened.

St Cuthbert's, Darlington's parish church, 1894. The gate piers and the churchyard walls were built in 1791, reputedly from the stones of a demolished vicarage that had once stood in its south-west corner.

On 7 May 1585, a fierce fire burned down 273 houses in Darlington, including much of High Row and Skinnergate. Little remained except St Cuthbert's Church. This interior view is a fine example of its beauty.

St Cuthbert's Church

Darlington.

The Ring of Eight was recast and rehung in a new frame by Messrs. Gillett & Johnston Ltd. The Bells were Rededicated on 25ᵗʰ March 1937. by the Vicar.

Nᵒ	Note	Inscriptions.	Weights Cwts Qrs Lbs		
1	F	Cast by John Warner & Sons, London. The gift of Joseph Pease Esquire. to complete the chime, 1866.	4	2	18
2	E	ditto.	4	3	12
3	D	Lester & Pack of London, Fecit 1755.	5	0	4
4	C	Mears & Stainbank Founders, London 1866. Restoration of St Cuthbert's Church when this bell, the third, and tenor bell were recast.	5	3	24
5	B♭	Lester & Pack of London, Fecit. Andrew Wood - Curate. Wm. Hall & Thos. Darnton & Wm. Duck & Ing. Brown. Churchwardens, 1755.	7	1	23
6	A	G. Mears & Cᵒ Founders, London. 1864	9	0	5
7	G	Lester & Pack of London, Fecit. Andrew Wood - Curate. Fras. Holmes, Robt. Westall, Mark Jeffrey, Richd. Southern. Churchwardens, 1760.	12	2	0
8	F	G. Mears & Cᵒ Founders, London, 1864. "The Ring of 8 was recast and rehung in the year of the Coronation of King George VI 1937." Vicar - W.C. Jordan. Churchwardens W.G. Chandler. W.E. Watson. G. Miners. G.H. Dawson.	18	0	14
			67	2	16

On each bell "Recast by Gillett & Johnston Croydon, 1937."

Vicar - The Rev. W.C. Jordan. M.A.

GILLETT & JOHNSTON L.
BELLFOUNDERS & LIRE FREE

Joseph Pease donated a ring of eight bells to St Cuthbert's Church in 1866. They were recast, rehung in another frame and rededicated on 25 March 1937.

Six of St Cuthbert's bells are going away to be recast, January 1937. The largest, the tenor bell, weighs 16¾ cwt. The bell on the extreme right is dated 1755.

Messrs O'Neill, father and son, removed and replaced the weathervane on St Cuthbert's spire, 20 September 1926. Behind them stands the verger, Mr J. Horsley, who assisted.

BRITAIN IN OLD PHOTOGRAPHS

To order any of these titles please telephone our distributor, Littlehampton Book Services on 01903 721596
For a catalogue of these and our other titles please ring Regina Schinner on 01453 731114